CLASS BOOK

Finding Out 2

David Paul

HEINEMANN

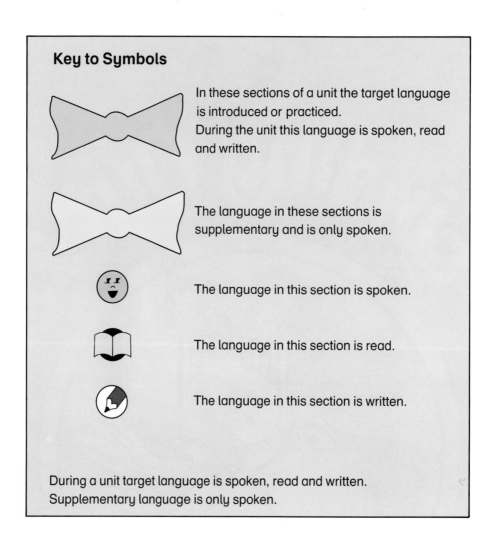

Key to Symbols

In these sections of a unit the target language is introduced or practiced.
During the unit this language is spoken, read and written.

The language in these sections is supplementary and is only spoken.

The language in this section is spoken.

The language in this section is read.

The language in this section is written.

During a unit target language is spoken, read and written.
Supplementary language is only spoken.

Author's acknowledgments

The author would like to thank:

Everyone at Heinemann for their encouragement, advice and hard work, especially **Mary Charrington**, **Sue Bale** and **Yvonne de Henseler**.

Chris Riddell and **Shireen Nathoo** for the lovely artwork and design.

Junko Fuwa for making it all possible with the original artwork.

James Barrow, **Debbie Owen** and **Paul Williams** for their advice and support in the early stages.

Richard Walker, **Marcus Boll** and **Barton Armstrong** for tightening up the theory and helping with the Teacher's Book.

All the teachers and staff at **David English House** who have believed in the course, and contributed so many useful suggestions during the eight years that it was developed and tested in the classroom.

Think of an Animal

Old Macdonald

quack

woof

Old Macdonald has 4 ducks
o͞o ar o͞o ar o͞w
1 duck, 2 ducks, 3 ducks, 4
o͞o ar o͞o ar o͞w
Quack, quack, quack. Quack, quack, quack
Old Macdonald has 4 ducks
o͞o ar o͞o ar o͞w

moo

cluck

Old Macdonald has 4 cows
o͞o ar o͞o ar o͞w
1 cow, 2 cows, 3 cows, 4
o͞o ar o͞o ar o͞w
Mo͞o mo͞o mo͞o. Mo͞o mo͞o mo͞o
Old Macdonald has 4 cows
o͞o ar o͞o ar o͞w

croak

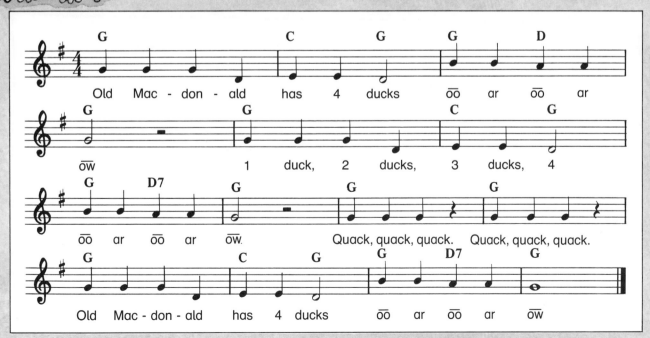

Old Mac - don - ald has 4 ducks o͞o ar o͞o ar

o͞w 1 duck, 2 ducks, 3 ducks, 4

o͞o ar o͞o ar o͞w. Quack, quack, quack. Quack, quack, quack.

Old Mac - don - ald has 4 ducks o͞o ar o͞o ar o͞w

9

You are a dog.

woof

moo

croak

1

2

3

Team Mime

Exercise

Are you a fox?

——— , — — .

Are you a frog?

——— , — , — — .

——— — — — — — ?

, — — — .

Dictation

1 — — —

2 — — —

3 — — — —

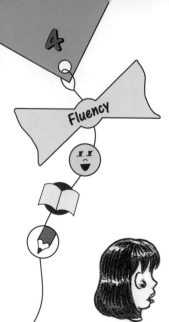

Is it a frog?

No, it isn't.

What is it?

It's a rabbit.

Is it gray and yellow?

No, it isn't.

What color is it?

It's black and white.

Colors Song

Red and white and pink and green
Orange and black and blue
Brown and yellow
Brown and yellow
Gray and purple too

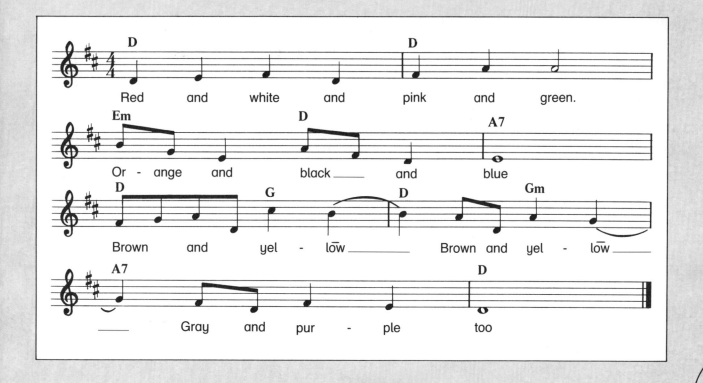

Red and white and pink and green.

Or - ange and black ___ and blue

Brown and yel - low ___ Brown and yel - low

___ Gray and pur - ple too

Exercise

Is it brown and white?

_____ , _____ _____ .

Is it green and blue?

_____ , _____ _____ , .

_____?

_____' _____ and _____ .

Dictation

1 __ _____ _____

2 __ _____ _____

3 __ _____ _____

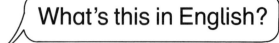
What's this in English?

It's a house.

What color is it?

It's red and white.

What's that in English?

It's a tree.

What color is it?

It's red, yellow and brown.

Touch and Point

Exercise

What's _____ __ _____ ?

_____ , _____ _____ _____ .

_____ , _____ _____ _____ _____ ?

_____ , _____ _____ _____ .

Dictation

1 _____ __ __ ?

2 _____ _____ __ __ ?

3 _____ , _____ _____ _____ ?

4 _____ , _____ _____ _____ ?

Ten Little Elephants

1 little, 2 little, 3 little elephants
4 little, 5 little, 6 little elephants
7 little, 8 little, 9 little elephants
10 little elephant boys

10 little, 9 little, 8 little elephants
7 little, 6 little, 5 little elephants
4 little, 3 little, 2 little elephants
1 little elephant girl

10 little, 20 little, 30 little elephants
40 little, 50 little, 60 little elephants
70 little, 80 little, 90 little elephants
100 little elephant boys

100 little, 90 little, 80 little elephants
70 little, 60 little, 50 little elephants
40 little, 30 little, 20 little elephants
10 little elephant girls

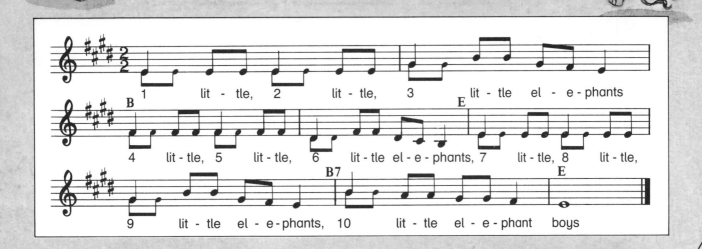

25

What _____ _____ ?

_____ , _____ _____ _____ .

_____ _____ _____ _____ ?

_____ _____ _____ _____ .

1 _____ _____ _____

2 _____ _____ _____

3 _____ _____ _____

houses

buses

octopuses

hippopotamuses

Counting Cards

Exercise

What _____ _____ ?

_____ _____ _____ _____ .

_____ _____ _____ _____ ?

_____ _____ _____ _____ .

Dictation

1 _____ _____ _____ .

2 _____ _____ _____ .

3 _____ _____ _____ .

4 _____ _____ _____ .

Exercise

Are they hōrses?

___ , ___ ___ .

___ ___ seals?

___ , ___ ___ ___ .

What ___ ___ ?

___ ___ ___ ___ .

Dictation

1 ___ ___ ___ ?

3 ___ , ___ ___ , .

3 ___ ___ ___ ?

4 ___ ___ ___ .

Exercise

_____ _____ red and white?

_____ , _____ _____ _____ .

_____ _____ blue and gray?

_____ , _____ _____ _____ , _____ .

What _____ ___ _____ ?

_____ ___ ___ _____ _____ .

Dictation

1 _____ , ___ ___ _____ _____ .

2 _____ , ___ ___ _____ .

3 _____ , ___ ___ _____ _____ .

4 _____ , ___ ___ _____ .

5 _____ , ___ ___ _____ _____ .

ea

ar

Words

er

11

Exercise

| | | x | | |

| | | n | n | | |
| | l | | | | |

| | | | h | | |

| | | | m | | |

| | | c | c | |
| | l | | | |

| | | | g | | |

| | | p | | t | | |

46

100 - 1,000

101, 102, 103, 104, 105, 106

Bingo

Exercise

| | | | | | r | m | |

| | | t | | |

| | | | k |

| | | l | | |

| | | t | | |

| | u | d | | |

Dictation

1 _____ _____ _____

2 _____ _____ _____

3 _____ _____ _____

Word Dominoes

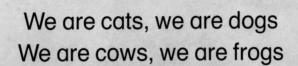

We are the World

We are cats, we are dogs
We are cows, we are frogs

We are the world, we are the children
We are the world, we are the children

We are doctors, we are sailors
We are teachers, we are farmers

We are the world, we are the children
We are the world, we are the children

We are ducks, we are bees
We are chickens, we are seals

We are the world, we are the children
We are the world, we are the children

We are cats! we are dogs! We are cows! we are frogs! We are the world, _____ we are the child - ren

We are the world, _____ we are the child - ren

Reading Check List

1 dogs

2 books

3 houses

4 yellow

5 brown

6 teacher

7 dentist

8 mailman

9 What color are they?

10 They are blue and green.

11 They are horses.

12 They are peaches.

13 What does he do?

14 He's a farmer.

15 She's a doctor.

16 He's a fisherman.

Heinemann English Language Teaching
A division of Reed Educational and Professional Publishing Limited
Halley Dourt, Jordan Hill, Oxford OX2 8EJ

OXFORD MADRID FLORENCE ATHENS PRAGUE SAO PAULO MEXICO CITY
CHICAGO PORTSMOUTH (NH) TOKYO SINGAPORE KUALA LUMPUR
MELBOURNE AUCKLAND JOHANNESBURG IBADAN GABORONE

ISBN 0 435 29024X

First published 1991

FINDING OUT 2 consists of:

Class Book	ISBN 0 435	29024X
Home Book	ISBN 0 435	290258
Teacher's Book	ISBN 0 435	290266
Cassette	ISBN 0 435	290274
Cards	ISBN 0 435	290452

Designed by Shireen Nathoo
Illustrated by Chris Riddell

Produced by Mandarin Offset, Hong Kong
Printed in Hong Kong

96 97 98 99 10 9 8 7 6 5 4